Master My Money

Master My Money

16 Steps To Solve Your Money Problems & Create A Foundation For Financial Freedom

By Dr. Dominiqué N. Reese

Published by

Reese Publishing
Los Angeles, California
ReeseFinancialServices.com

Master My Money

Published by
Reese Publishing
Los Angeles, California
ReeseFinancialServices.com
Copyright © 2015 by Dominiqué Reese

Library of Congress Control Number: 2015945054

ISBN-13: 978-0-9963386-1-5

Cover Design by LaNoya Corley

Interior Design by Valerie J. Lewis Coleman

Edited by Carol Lane

Printed in the United States of America

Disclaimer

This book is designed to provide accurate and reliable information on the subject of personal finance. It is intended solely as a source of information for readers and is not intended to substitute for professional advice. If the reader needs advice concerning the evaluation and management of specific legal or financial risks or liabilities, such as bankruptcy or tax matters, he or she should seek the help of a licensed or certified or knowledgeable professional. The author and publisher specifically disclaim any liability, loss or risk that is incurred as an outcome, directly or indirectly, through the use and application of any content of this work.

Master My Money

Praise for Master My Money...

"Upon meeting Dr. Reese and working with her on my MoneyWise Empowerment Tour, she demonstrated a magnetic energy and passion for educating everyday people about money. She is steadily crafting her skill to connect and be relatable with audiences, to deliver sound, informative and practical financial information and be a leading authority in her field of personal finance. If you are ready to take your financial knowledge to the next level, be empowered with the tools you need to manage better your financial life and feel good about it, then you are ready to master your money and *Master My Money: 16 Steps To Solve Your Money Problems & Create A Foundation For Financial Freedom* is just the book you need to help you get started."

—Kelvin Boston
Best-Selling Author, Financial Journalist, Entrepreneur

"When it comes to money management, books and approaches are a dime a dozen. Seldom can you find a book that is down to earth, practical and filled with strategies that ANYONE can leverage to experience a financial shift. What I enjoyed about Dr. Reese's *Master My Money* is the simple approach to shifting the way you manage money. Her plan is easy to follow, easy to stick to and easy for being able to see your money management shift so that you can experience wealth in your lifetime. I highly recommend this easy read for the person who is ready to master their money!"

—Darnyelle A. Jervey
Award-Winning Business Coach & CEO Incredible One Enterprises

7

"As a tax consultant, writer and speaker, I have conducted many financial literacy programs. I'm a strong believer in providing down-to-earth and straight to the point financial advice to my audience. I would highly recommend this book for anybody living paycheck to paycheck. This book gets straight to the point on what you need to do to make the most of your money. This book will empower you and your family!"

—Jamaal Solomon
EA, MST, Owner, J.S. Tax Corporation, Author of A Good Guy's Tax Journey Part 1: Tax Tips on How to Deal With the IRS and Live to Fight Another Day

"If I had this book when I was 16 or even 21, I would have been ahead of the game in building wealth. This book will be the reason why a lot of people become wealthy, financially sound and will help families build substantial wealth. Especially Chapter 2! Thank you for your financial brilliance Dominiqué Reese."

—Amir Windom
Grammy Award Winning Record Executive

Acknowledgements

To God, thank You for Your grace, mercy, guidance and love. Thank You for teaching me to trust in You, rather than my own understanding. Thank You Father, I love You.

To everyone who has ever wished me well, prayed for me, supported me and kept my best interest at heart, this book is for you. This is what you have motivated me to do. Thank you for keeping me honest, accountable and down-to-earth.

To my son, Ya'ir Whitney Reese Payton, Mommy did it. Now, you must teach those who come after you.

To my family, thank you for loving me, through my good and my bad.

Master My Money

Master My Money
Table of Contents

Master My Money

Foreword

I met Dominiqué Reese where I meet most other financial experts of her caliber…in the trenches educating the community about financial literacy. For many years we would continuously cross paths at economic empowerment workshops, financial literacy panel discussions, and now on the shelves of bookstores. More than most I trust Dominiqué because she "gets it". She gets that it is not only important to deliver a crucial message assisting the masses on a path towards financial independence, but to possess the humility to deliver the message in a means that is desirably digestible. As important as a message may be it is no good if the people have no desire to consume it.

Dominiqué also gets the timeliness of this message. The world is increasingly becoming a "protest society". One can turn on the news at any time to see protests that are continuously increasing the demands of accountability on government, police, corporations, and more. Millions remain glued to television from election cycle to election cycle debating which candidate will be best suited to turn around this economy. Democrats state the government is not doing enough, while Republicans state the government is doing way too much. In all of the protesting and debating the one thing that gets lost is the focus on the necessity to improve upon oneself. It is very easy to point the finger at somebody else, but it takes true character to discern how your own actions fell short of hitting the mark towards helping the greater good and advancing our communities. While there are many things we can do to help the greater good advance such as voting, protesting, and spreading positive messages on Facebook...Dominiqué, like me, chooses to focus on creating individual economic empowerment movements within homes through the education of personal financial principles.

Yes...the greed of corporations played a tremendous role in crushing our economy and we must continue to press for laws and regulations not to allow the same thing to happen again. However, if more people had been properly educated on how to improve their credit and purchase homes responsibly this deficiency in our knowledge would not have been able to be exploited.

No...Eric Garner didn't deserve to die for selling loose cigarettes. I was just as mad as others the police officer wasn't indicted and I joined in the outcry. However, there are others out there who because they don't know the basic principles of entrepreneurship feel that selling loose cigarettes is a viable mean to earn a living. Can't we fight to be sure that irresponsible actions of police are properly penalized AND promote the principles of how to form a legitimate business?

Yes...I am just as mad as others that we are seeing the continuous growth of a $360 billion industry exploit our communities in the form of check cashing stores, payday lenders, rent-to-own stores, title loan establishments, cash-4-gold pawn shops, and pre-paid debit cards. As mad as I am they are exploiting the ignorance in our communities, I wish more would join me in being just as mad about our communities allowing that ignorance to exist. We can steal the customer base of all of these predators by empowering ourselves with an ability to budget, build credit, manage debt responsibly, and learn the principles of financial literacy. We make all of the financial predators that plague our communities go broke if we simply follow the principles outlined in this brilliant piece of work that Dominiqué has put together.

Ignorance of financial principles that are so vital to the economic vitality of our country is no longer acceptable. If I may be so bold, high-minded financial experts who lack the ability/humility to talk to the masses on their level are also no longer acceptable. So I am proud that my friend decided to take on a topic in a way that makes it as simple as it really is. So put away your fear and your inhibitions because *Master My Money* will eliminate all of your excuses as to why you can't budget, improve your credit, eliminate your debt, and much more. There is nothing wrong with being ignorant, but there is something wrong with remaining ignorant.

Thanks, Dominiqué for helping to build a smarter America.

Sincerely,

Ryan Mack

Master My Money

Introduction

Thank you.

Thank you for entrusting me to lead you to a new space in your financial life. To a place where you can begin to create a foundation of wealth for you and your family. This book is an important part of your financial journey—one that you can rely on, and return to whenever you need guidance, information, or inspiration.

I wrote this book because I wanted to be able to reach more people with my Master My Money personal financial coaching system. It's a proven, ten-step process that empowers you to get your financial house in order, and stop living paycheck to paycheck (or client to client, if you're a business owner). The process will enable you to take your savings to the next level, and make the most of your hard-earned money.

Although I am a personal financial coach and strategist, and work with clients across the country, I can only reach a limited number of people one-on-one. So, I determined that writing this book would help me achieve my mission to change financial lives, one budget at a time.

You don't have to brave this journey alone. If you decide to take the next step in your journey and seek private coaching, you can reach me directly via email and, eventually, by phone. But even if you never take that step, I want to ensure your financial success. The process in this book is the same process I use to guide my private coaching clients.

I want you to become so good at managing your everyday financial life that you truly master your money. Think about it...how many things can you actually master that will make a difference in the quality of your life? Your money is one of those things.

Aren't you ready for more? Are you tired of having the same experiences with your money? Tired of overdrawing your account? Robbing Peter to pay Paul? Barely making it to the next paycheck? Spending more than you know you should, but feeling like you deserve to spend because you work so hard?

I get it. I understand. I have been in all of those financial situations. And, using the system I've created and perfected over the years, I've successfully escaped them. I speak, educate, and coach from that personal experience. These strategies have worked for me. And I know that if you implement them, they can work for you, too.

Money is behavioral. And ultimately, it's our behavior that dictates our financial success. Think about that. Everything you do (or don't do) in your financial life contributes to your financial success or failure. So it logically follows that changing your financial life can be as simple as changing your behavior. That's what my back-to-basics approach is designed to do.

What are the basics? They include the things that we've all heard of, but may never have mastered: our mindset and our goals, for example. Are you able to think positively about your financial capabilities? What about setting goals for any area of your life? Have you accomplished what you'd like to with your money?

Because you're reading this book, it's likely you haven't yet mastered these areas. But that will change.

This is your opportunity to learn techniques that will never steer you wrong. Even if you stray or find yourself in over your head months from now, you will have learned strategies that will enable you to resolve your situation. That's the purpose of this book: to equip you with the tools and information that will give you control over your money, no matter your income level, or the severity of your situation.

Ultimately, I'll teach you how to create the foundation you need for your financial life. Then, when you're faced with an unexpected financial situation, your foundation won't be jeopardized - because you are prepared.

Imagine that.

Imagine operating from a place of peace about your money, knowing that handling that emergency won't put you into an overdraft situation. That taking a spontaneous trip to the outlet mall won't stress you for the next two weeks. That loaning $500 to a friend or family member won't put you in a vulnerable position, even if it isn't repaid. That taking your family out to a favorite restaurant won't cause you worry and headaches.

When you know your financial house is not in order, these kinds of everyday money situations can cause a great deal of stress. But, when we operate confidently with our money, we don't need to worry about such things. We learn the real meaning of "don't sweat the small stuff." What a relief.

I want to move you to that place. I want you to master your money, so you can enjoy a peace like no other. I want to equip you with strategies and information you can refer to at any time. I want you to have the power to get back on track if you skip a beat.

So how will we do that?

You'll start by reading each chapter of this book, in order, the first time around. When completing the exercises, write directly in the book. It has been designed to enable you to keep all your important financial information right here, so you don't risk misplacing loose papers with your notes. Read the instructions for each exercise closely, and follow them.

Remember, this system is tried and true. It works when clients follow it as instructed. If you have questions about anything in this book, email me at: dominique@reesefinancialservices.com.

Ready? Let's get started.

Step 1
Identify Your "Why Now?"

Over the years, I've worked with hundreds of clients. And I've learned that there are two main reasons someone decides it's time to make a change, and seeks financial help from a professional:

1. They've had a change of heart.

2. They're facing—or are about to face—an actual crisis.

As a personal financial coach and strategist, I've found both of these situations frequently bring about an urgent change in your priorities. That change quickly causes you to make a significant shift in your financial habits. I call this your "Why Now."

It's important to determine your own "Why Now." You can do it by answering this simple question: Why are you reading this book?

Are you fed up with living paycheck to paycheck? Tired of being broke? Do you see your situation becoming much worse, very soon? Have you already hit rock bottom, and simply can't take it anymore? Are you ready to master your money?

Your "Why Now" might be prompted by a certain time of year, or an upcoming life event. Did you make a New Year's resolution to focus on your money? Are you planning to get married? Did you recently have a baby? Are you concerned you or your spouse will be laid off from work?

Your "Why Now" can also be the result of a shift in priorities and values. Maybe you've decided you want to travel, or experience life a bit more. Perhaps you're simply tired of watching your credit card debt grow. It's even possible you've noticed the stress of your financial situation is impacting your health, and decided you must make a change.

My why now was prompted by a life-changing event, but lasted over time. I had gotten laid off from Merrill Lynch as a financial advisor, making close to $60,000 at the age of 23. Sadly enough, I didn't have any savings (I'll get to that shortly) but I had severance. I decided to start my own business months later, after taking a vacation to Paris for ten days. Yep! I sure did; no job and all! Upon my return, CommuniTree, LLC was born. It was my financial education company where I offered one-on-one money management counseling. Now, I didn't just have personal expenses and household expenses, I had business expenses too. Severance pay was about to come to an end, but I had some money coming, so I didn't sweat it too much. I was expecting $50,000, as part of a settlement due to my dad's death when I was two-years old. Nevertheless, I was waiting on this money and I had a plan for what to do with it, once I got it. Did I stick to the plan? Of course not! I had never before received that much money at one time. I definitely used the money to catch up on bills, pay off debt, to cover my living expenses and invest in my business. But I also spent money on traveling, unnecessary expenses, helping family and God knows what else! Sad to say, but I really can't remember! It's a blur. I do know I didn't do nearly as much as I had planned. I realized month after month, that even though I had more money, I didn't behave any differently. I behaved the same as I did when I was bringing home a salary. I hadn't necessarily improved my habits. It was the same behavior that led me to have no savings when I got laid off. Even though I had lots of knowledge about money, knowledge wasn't enough. I was financially literate and still behaved illiterately. This was a problem. I needed to be able to take action on my knowledge, to implement a behavior that would lead to outcomes I desired. Favorable outcomes. This is when my "why now" became so ever crystal clear. I snapped out of it and told myself I didn't want to go back to corporate. I wanted to pursue my entrepreneurial endeavors and work for myself. I was steadily investing in my business and money was steadily dwindling. I understood that I needed to know where I was putting my money. I needed to get discipline, make better decisions and get on a system for how I managed things, instead of just making decisions because I knew I had the money. I'll tell you, I learned that just because you can, doesn't mean you should! Remember that. Privately, I felt so embarrassed that I had gotten myself into this situation. Here I was; a former financial advisor who wasn't disciplined with her money, who didn't follow her own plan, who helped other people with their money, but couldn't help herself. This didn't feel good. I felt like a hypocrite. Worst of all, I *knew* better, but didn't do better. So, I made the change. I truly started to behave differently. I decided I would start tracking my every penny, so I knew where my hard-earned money was going. It wasn't enough to say, "Oh, it's in my head." I needed to write it down and make it real. My "why now" jumped out at me every day, on my pocket tracker. I had an everyday reminder of why it was so important to be attentive to my money. I learned so much about myself, so much about my spending habits and patterns, my weaknesses and strength, where I spent the most money and the least, how often I bought this or that. I got into an intimate relationship with my money. As I learned, the numbers were telling a story and they never lie. I started to change that story, the day I began tracking. And it felt so good. I was starting to master my money, one purchase at a time, one day at a time.

The system you'll learn in this book will help you define and gather the information you need to make better decisions about your money. But it all starts with understanding your "Why Now." Your "Why Now" is your constant reminder of the reasons you're undertaking this process of change.

You'll refer back to it any time you get discouraged in your journey, or make another mistake. (And you will make more mistakes. The difference will be that you'll know how to correct them quickly, without letting them jeopardize your wealth foundation.)

Whatever your "Why Now" may be, it's important to define and understand it. In the space below, share why you've decided that now is the time to take action toward improving your personal financial situation:

_____

_____

_____

_____

_____

_____

_____

Having a change of heart about your personal financial situation is a more positive reason for making a change than facing a crisis. (If you're in a crisis, your situation is already beyond your control.) But they're both an invaluable first step in your path forward.

Money Master Principle #1

Adopt motivating money and wealth mindsets

Step 2
Recover From Your Money Downfall

Your financial situation can and will improve. You can recover from money problems, no matter how severe they may be.

Financial issues are different from other types of problems, like illness. Once our health starts to deteriorate, there are usually only certain things we can do to improve it. And we may never fully recover. Don't get me wrong; I'm a firm believer in holistic methods and homeopathic remedies. And I've heard the studies of people resurrecting their health, and transitioning from "dead" to "alive." But here, I'm speaking more generally. When we learn we have a disease or illness, or are at risk for one, we can take steps to improve the situation. But there are no certainties.

With money and wealth, we know we can recover. We can hit rock bottom, then make changes that move us beyond where we began, and help us soar to financial success, as we define it.

What we commonly refer to as "rags to riches" stories are much more than just stories. They're the real experiences of people just like you.

Once you've decided that you *can* do better, *want* to do better, and *want* to seek the abundance awaiting you, your next step is deciding to seek help. Acknowledging that you can benefit from guidance and discipline can be difficult, but it's very necessary. (Of course, if you're facing an actual crisis, making that decision can be a bit easier.)

Few of us are comfortable voluntarily admitting that our financial house is not in order. In our society, sharing that type of information is often taboo. Money is very personal. And many of us consider our financial mistakes and challenges to be embarrassing, and a poor reflection of who we are and what we stand for. Just like I did.

However, I assure you that even the wealthiest individuals make ill-informed financial decisions that don't lead to the best outcome. But it's important to acknowledge that each financial decision is an individual choice, made one at a time. If you begin to consider each decision you make about your money more carefully, you begin to change your mindset. That change will impact the actions you take with your money.

Eventually, you'll begin to make informed, sound decisions consistently. That consistency will create a positive impact on your finances, and lead to the outcomes you desire.

You will have moments of doubt and discouragement. So remember, simply getting started is a defining milestone for your future success. Waiting another day won't make your situation any better. So stop beating yourself up. You've chosen NOW to do something to change your personal financial situation. You've taken that difficult, vital first step.

Yesterday's actions don't matter as much as today's and tomorrow's. Remember, change happens one decision at a time. One day at a time.

"Money is a tool to use for ownership, control and legacy. Don't work for it, let it work for you."
                                                    —Davu (New York)

Master My Money

Money Master Davu

Brother Davu is an astute, Afro-centric conscious business owner, community activist and role model. He believed in wealth building and came to me with the mindset of a wealthy warrior. However, Davu's challenge was in managing all that he had. He had money here, money there, an account for this, an account for that, business money here, personal there. To say the least, he was all over the place and needed a system for managing his financial life, in addition to filling some holes in his financial foundation. Davu was stubborn and liked the method to his madness, but needed a coach to whip him into shape and give him the winning strategies to take his finances to the next level. He already had so much in place, it just needed some dire organization, and replenishment. I suggested he begin tracking because he was spending way too much money. Although he had it to spend, he needed that money to go towards the holes in his foundation, holes he didn't necessarily see before working with me. Ultimately, he gave in to tracking and while he hated having to jot down his expenses in the tracker I gave him, he loved that he wasn't spending like he used to. He was able to redirect funds towards his protection needs and save more towards his financial future. Further, I referred Davu to an Enrolled Agent, Jamaal Solomon, in my Trusted Advisor Network (available to all clients) to handle his chaotic tax situation. The system was being built for Davu to better manage his personal and business financial affairs like the true Money Master he was.

Master My Money

Step 3
Understand What's Coming In and Going Out

Most of us can quote, without hesitation, the amount of money we bring in every month. However, when asked about our total monthly expenses, the response is usually quite different.

In my experience helping people build solid wealth foundations, the vast majority of the time, they can't tell me their average monthly expenses. More often than not, they'll start to simply list their monthly bills. "Well, my rent is $1,250, my car is $250..." and so on. And that's where I have to stop them.

I remind them that my original question was, "What is your total average monthly expenditure?" At this point, I usually hear one of three responses:

1. "I don't know. Somewhere around..." Then they quote a number close to their total average monthly *income*.

2. "Let me think…" They then start to enumerate their expenses again, one-by-one, and add them together to come to a final total.

3. "About $200-$500 *more* than my income."

Although I ask the question to gather data about my client, it's also an exercise I employ to learn about the client's habits. It gives me an opportunity to see how familiar the individual is with their income and expenses, and ultimately, their spending. I've concluded that quoting our income is much easier for us because it's a fixed number that, for the most part, is consistent. Our income and expenses play an integral role in our budget because they actually *are* the budget.

When individuals hesitate or stumble when quoting their income, it's usually because part of it is variable. They may have a commission-based part-time job, or own a small business. But the majority of us bring home the same paycheck on a regular basis.

Quoting our expenses is more difficult for several reasons. We don't usually pay all our expenses in one lump sum, at regular intervals. Also, we have multiple expenses to manage, with varying amounts, due at various times. That variability doesn't provide a stable view of our total expenses.

Understanding total expenses takes more work than understanding income. We have to list each one, and then add them together to reach a total. And, that total will likely change from month to month. Some expenses are fixed, others are variable. Some are short-term, others are longer term.

An expense figure is also harder to quote because often we're simply not in tune with how much we spend on a monthly basis. For some of us, we just know a bill is due, we pay it (or not), and move on to the next one. On top of that, we frequently incur other, singular expenses, like a birthday present or a dinner out. Those purchases pull money from our total monthly income, outside of what we normally anticipate.

Ultimately, it's critical to understand both your total average monthly income and your total average monthly expenses. Having a firm grip on these numbers gives you a much greater understanding of your personal financial situation. If you know what's coming in and going out, you'll be able to take better control of your finances. Now, let's put all of this talk to action!

Master My Money

Money Master Principle #2

Set and reset wealth-related goals

Master My Money

Step 4
Your Current Financial Situation

Do your best to fill in the numbers below. We're just creating a general idea of your income and expenses, so don't worry if you're unsure or a bit inaccurate. Just give it your best shot, from memory. (No cheating. Don't dig through past bills and statements!)

Category	Total Monthly	Months	Total Annually
Income:	$	x 12	$
Expenses:	$	x 12	$

Next, let's identify your current savings.

There are four types of savings: emergency fund savings, regular or goal-specific savings, investment savings and retirement savings. If you're saving money in any of these areas each month, fill in the amounts below. Take your best guess, and don't worry if you're not sure of the exact numbers. (Remember, no cheating!)

Monthly Savings	
Emergency Fund	$
Regular or Goal-Specific	$
Investment	$
Retirement	$
Total	$

What are the current balances in your savings accounts?

Current Savings Accounts Balances	
Emergency Fund	$
Regular or Goal-Specific	$
Investment	$
Retirement	$
Total	$

If you're not currently saving, why not?

_____

_____

_____

What is preventing you from saving? _____

_____

_____

Now, let's look at your debt.
Again, this is a high-level view, so don't worry about getting the numbers exactly right. Remember, right now you're simply sharing your numbers to create a basic understanding of your current financial standing.

Total Outstanding Debt Balances			
Type of Debt	No	Yes	If yes, how much?
Credit Card			
Store/Charge Card			
Student Loan			
Mortgage			
Auto Loan			
Tax Liabilities			
Medical Expenses			
Collection Agencies			
IOU to Relative/Friend			
Child Support			
Alimony			
Other Debts			
		Total	

Your debt utilization ratio.

Your debt utilization ratio is the amount of debt you're using compared to the amount of credit available to you.

For example, if you took out a student loan for $10,000 and your balance is $8,000, then your debt utilization for that loan is 80% ($8,000 ÷ $10,000 * 100%). You're using 80% of the credit (loan) available to you.

To calculate your utilization ratio, divide your balance by the amount available to you, then multiply the value by 100%. The percent means for every $1 of credit available to you, you're using (fill in the blank with the number from the percent) cents of it.

Another example: If you have a $1,000 credit card limit with a balance of $200, then your debt utilization is $200 ÷ $1000 = 0.20 * 100% = 20%. In other words, for every $1 of credit available to you, you're using $0.20.

Consider all of your debt, the credit limits available to you and the balances (amount used) for each debt.

Master My Money

Debt	Amount Used	Amount Available
Total		

Divide the total amount used by the total amount available and then multiply by 100% to calculate your debt utilization.

My debt utilization is _____.

Debt Utilization	What does this mean?	It is suggested that you...
>43%	You don't want to be here!	reduce aggressively
31%-43%	Uh-oh, you're heading to a place you don't want to be!	reduce moderately aggressively
30%	It's okay to be here.	reduce
0-29%	This is where you want to be!	reduce with ease

Moving right along to credit.

Three main credit bureaus are used by lenders, credit card companies and others to learn about your creditworthiness: Equifax, Experian and TransUnion.

Let's do a quick credit review.

When was the last time you checked your credit report?

_____

_____

Do you know your credit score?   Yes_____ No_____

What is your approximate credit score? If you don't know, guess. _____

Let's talk protection for a moment.
Answer the following questions to the best of your knowledge:

Do you have life insurance?   Yes_____ No_____

If so, how much is your total death benefit? $_____

How much is your premium? $_____

How often do you pay the premium? Circle one

     Monthly   Quarterly   Semi-annually   Annually

Is the policy term or permanent? _____

If term, when does the policy expire? _____

Do you have car insurance?   Yes_____ No_____

Do you have renter's insurance?   Yes_____ No_____

Do you have business insurance?   Yes_____ No_____

Do you have health insurance?   Yes_____ No_____

Do you have a living will?   Yes_____ No_____

Do you have a trust?   Yes____ No____

Do you have health proxies?   Yes____ No____

Do you have advance directives?   Yes____ No____

Good job!

Take a moment to reflect on how you felt completing the last few pages. Use the space below to assess how you felt about seeing your current financial situation in written form.

How do you feel about your responses?

_____

_____

_____

Are you satisfied with them?

_____

_____

_____

If not, what do you want to change? If yes, what do you want to remain the same?

_____

_____

_____

Did you have more "no" answers than "yes" answers? Or more "yes" answers than "no" answers?

_____

_____

_____

Did you have a hard time recalling some of the information to answer the questions?

_____

_____

_____

Do you feel in tune with your current financial situation, now that you've completed this exercise?

_____

_____

_____

If so, how? If not, why not?

_____

_____

_____

What section of the assessment was most striking for you and why?

_____

What section are you most proud of, if any?

_____

_____

_____

What section do you feel you need the most help with restoring or creating?

_____

_____

_____

Remember, the answers you provided here are based on your memory. We'll be getting much more detailed soon. This high-level assessment is meant to help put you "in the know" about your current personal financial situation. It's just the beginning of your money story. The great thing is that you have the power to change that story. Getting "in the know" is about awareness. You can't fix something if you don't know it's broken.

Finally, don't be too hard on yourself. You've done the difficult part; you've "faced the music" as I like to say. It's not always easy to do, but it's incredibly brave. It's the beginning of the process of changing your personal financial situation.

Money Master Principle #3

Maintain and balance a household budget

Master My Money

Step 5

The Money Plan

We've done a high-level assessment of where you currently stand in your financial life. You've faced the music, and you now know what you have, and what you need. You understand how much your debt is costing you, and how much you're saving. You know if you're out of touch with your credit profile, and you've stated your goals.

Now, it's time to get excited about your money again because you're going to begin to move beyond your past mistakes or challenges, and start to see the light at the end of the tunnel. You'll now connect your financial needs with a solution. Remember, nobody's financial situation is so bad that they can't recover. Your situation is fixable, and that fix begins today.

The assessment you completed covered six main areas. Working with hundreds of people has taught me that building the foundation of wealth stems from these six core areas of our financial lives. When we are able to master our money in these areas, we begin to see the changes we want to create become reality. Given that, you may ask, how do I master these areas? Simply put, you'll master them by establishing and repeating new, better behaviors. To put another away, you'll practice. You know the saying, "practice makes perfect." While it applies to learning the piano, it's also very true for managing your money.

If you don't want to live paycheck to paycheck to paycheck anymore, you have to change your behavior. If you are sick and tired of being broke, you have to change your behavior. Money management is behavioral. Our bank accounts are a reflection of our behavior. So, in order to change our money, we have to change our minds, and ultimately, our behavior.

The six core areas of your wealth foundation are noted below:

1. Mindsets and goals
2. Total income and expenses (budget)
3. Savings
4. Debt
5. Credit
6. Protection

While everyone may have different financial needs, the solutions that address those needs are generally similar. The six areas we addressed in our assessment correspond to six practical solutions:

1. Shift our mindset, set goals
2. Increase income, decrease expenses
3. Save more, save frequently
4. Reduce and/or eliminate debt
5. Improve credit profile
6. Acquire protection

More than likely, a combination of these six common solutions will move you toward becoming a better steward of your money and ultimately, closer to building the wealth foundation you deserve.

When you live paycheck-to-paycheck, it's usually because of one of or a combination of the following reasons:

1. You lack motivating mindsets and accountability to your goals.
2. You're living outside of your means. *(You spend more than you earn.)*
3. You have little or no savings to fall back on, or you're simply not saving at all.
4. Debt payments consume most of your income.
5. Your credit is in poor condition.
6. You don't have proper protection.

Do any of the reasons in the table below apply to your personal financial situation? Circle all that apply.

A solution is available for each reason to help you understand the steps you'll need to take to improve your personal financial situation.

REASON	SOLUTION
Living outside of your means	Increase income, decrease expenses
Little or no savings	Save more, save frequently
Overwhelming debt payments	Reduce debt
Poor credit	Improve credit
Lack proper protection.	Acquire proper coverage
Lack motivating mindsets and accountability to your goals	Shift your mindset and set S.M.A.R.T. goals

Simple enough, right? While it's definitely not rocket science, we can't discount how challenging the decisions we have to make when improving our finances can be. While those choices aren't easy, you'll become more disciplined with some practice. Soon, you'll find that following a new system becomes routine. Paycheck-to-paycheck living transforms into a new, more positive habit, one that I call "paycheck-to-paycheck abundance."

Your plan moving forward is to adopt and integrate these solutions into your financial life, so that you can stop living paycheck-to-paycheck, and achieve your goals. In the next few chapters, you'll dive deeper into your personal financial situation so you can see how we begin to implement these solutions. We'll take a look at your financial history over the past thirty days, examine your income and expenses in more detail, start tracking your spending, learn how much you can afford to save, and reduce your debt in a way that makes sense for your budget, lifestyle, and comfort level.

"An eye-opening experience! At times, a hard pill to swallow, but a much needed self-exploration."
—Besy & Lamine (California)

Money Masters Besy & Lamine

This fabulous couple was so fabulous they'd partake in the lap of luxury we call Costcos! Buying in bulk for two people was simply their thing! However, we know just how tempting Costcos can be, as they truly offer household goods that we all can use. But when the bill is to the tune of $700 a month for two, we scream loud and clear that 'Houston we have a problem." Besy and Lamine were one of my best couples to work with because they were coachable, yet asked questions when they didn't quite understand a strategy I built. They certainly had two incomes to meet their needs, but found themselves in that paycheck to paycheck cycle nevertheless. With ambitions of starting a family one day, savings and debt reduction was at the top of their list. I constructed a three-pronged strategy that allowed for a moderately aggressive debt reduction, intense savings and a reduction in their monthly expenses. With "newfound money" we were able to setup a savings strategy while reducing debt, as both were important to their success. Further, the education this couple acquired truly brightened their horizon. They gradually adopted wealth mindsets and truly began to *feel* financially free. Their behavior was changing before their very own eyes and so were the dollars in their bank account, and the balances on their credit card statements. Adopting motivating mindsets and implementing their custom strategies proved to be fruitful and worthwhile. Not only did they leave me with reduced debt, increased savings and lower monthly expenses, but they also consolidated separate and joint accounts to develop a manageable sustainable system for their new foundation of wealth.

Step 6

Mindsets and Goal Setting

Simply put, a goal is something you want to achieve. Because you're reading this book, it's clear you want to achieve something. So, what is it? Do you want to stop living paycheck-to-paycheck? Do you want to be free from financial stress? Do you want to spend with no worries? Do you want to save for a rainy day? Do you want to be debt free? Do you want to be confident enough about your personal financial situation that you can begin to invest? Do you want or need to adjust your savings so that, instead of sitting in cash, that money is working for you?

What is your financial desire(s)?

_____

_____

_____

_____

_____

Your current financial situation is the result of a specific set of financial behaviors or attitudes you hold. Do you know what that is? Give it some thought. Why do you think you end up in the financial situations you do? Are you too generous? Too frugal? Too loose with your money? Uninformed about the decisions you make? Ill-educated on how credit cards or other financial products work? Unaware of the consequences of specific behaviors? Too scared to try something new with your money?

Use the space below to jot your thoughts about why you find yourself in unfavorable financial situations.

_____

_____

_____

_____

_____

After considering why you find yourself in unfavorable financial situations, it's time to explore the role those reasons play in your money mindset. Your money mindset is simply what you believe about money. Some examples of mindsets are:

"I'd rather save something than nothing."

"I don't make enough money to save."

"I don't want to be restricted by a budget."

"Investing isn't for me, I don't know enough about it and I don't want to lose money."

"Insurance is just a way to get rich off the dead."

"I just want to be comfortable. As long as my bills are paid, I'm okay."

"I'll save when I _____."

"I know I want to do more with my money, but I'm not sure where to start or what to do."

"Financial Advisors aren't for me. I don't have enough money to get help and I can't afford it."

"I work hard. I like spending my money on what I want, when I want."

Which of these mindsets resonate with you?

_____

_____

_____

_____

_____

_____

_____

_____

Now that I've shared some common money mindsets, what are YOUR unique mindsets about money? Write your mindsets below:

1. _____
2. _____
3. _____

Look back at what you've written. Are these mindsets positive or negative? Positive mindsets are "motivating" mindsets, while negative mindsets are "limiting" mindsets. Of the three mindsets you listed, place an "M" next to those that are motivating and an "L" next to those that are limiting.

Do you have more motivating or limiting mindsets on your list? _____

How does that make you feel?

_____
_____
_____
_____
_____
_____
_____

If you have motivating mindsets on your list, you'll want to focus on supporting and maintaining them by coupling them with positive actions. For example, if you believe in saving something over nothing, follow up with a positive, affirming action, such as making regular deposits—of any size—in your savings account.

On the other hand, if you've found that you have more limiting mindsets than motivating ones, you'll want to consider the following:

1. Why do you have those mindsets? Take steps to change the behaviors that create and support them.

2. Create an opposing, motivating mindset for each limiting mindset you have. For example, if your mindset is, "I don't have enough money to save," an opposing motivating mindset could be, "I will review my expenses and see what I can reduce or eliminate so I can start saving."

3. Hire and work with a Financial Coach or Professional Daily Money Manager to help you understand and change your money mindset and adopt new behaviors.

Limiting mindsets are only as detrimental as we allow them to be. For some people, this can be very dangerous. For others, it can be harmless, as long as they're aware of the impact that mindset can have. Keep in mind that awareness doesn't always lead to changes in behavior. That's when action becomes even more important. To help you begin to take action, let's review each of the suggestions above, in more detail.

Money mindsets are born from our past, present and/or future. Think about where the money mindsets you listed came from. Were they born from experiences with money from your past, present, or future? All three?

Understanding the origins of your limiting mindsets can help you move beyond them. Some of us do what we saw our parents do. Some of us simply didn't know what to do, and made the best decisions we could with the information we had.

The following prompts can help you explore why you have the money mindsets you do, and where they originated.

Prompt 1:

Reflect upon a negative experience you've had with your money. Choose any experience that stands out the most for you. What happened? How did you respond? How did you feel? What specifically made you feel that way? Can you see yourself experiencing this again? How can you avoid negative experiences like this in the future?

_____

_____

_____

_____

_____
_____
_____
_____
_____
_____

Prompt 2:

Reflect upon a positive experience you've had with your money. Choose any experience that stands out the most for you. What happened? How did you respond? How did you feel? What specifically made you feel that way? Can you see yourself experiencing this again? How can you replicate positive experiences like this in the future?

_____
_____
_____
_____
_____
_____
_____
_____
_____

Master My Money

Expressing your thoughts about a negative and positive financial memory can make it easier to understand your money mindsets. What you believe about your money has been shaped by the experiences you've had, what you have or haven't been taught, and what you've seen others do with their money. We'll reference these mindsets from time to time, simply to remind us of where we want to be and where we don't want to be. These money memories serve as powerful motivation for achieving your financial goals.

When shifting from a limiting mindset to a motivating mindset, you always want to speak in the affirmative about your aspirations. Consider the limiting mindsets you have, and then their opposing, motivating mindset. Use the statements below to help you speak in the affirmative about money, and to consider the motivating mindsets you want to adopt moving forward:

1. Although I am not good at _____, I will work on improving it to accomplish my goal of/to _____.

2. I will improve _____
   _____

3. I am good at _____ and will continue to improve_____
   _____

4. I will save $_____ every _____ for the next _____.

5. I will learn more about _____, so I can grow in my financial life.

6. Even though the thought of _____ scares me, I will address it head on, so that it doesn't prevent me from creating a solid wealth foundation.

7. I will not become hostage to my debt, and will strive to pay off $_____ in debt before the last day of the month of _____ in the year____.

8. My credit score is important to creating a solid wealth foundation, so I will monitor my credit more closely throughout the year. I can check my credit at least once a year for free at <u>AnnualCreditReport.com</u>.

9. Life insurance is critical to building wealth. I will learn more about the types of insurance available and work toward securing the best policy for me.

10. I will reduce one expense this week/month. It will be_____.

Now that we have addressed your mindset and considered the mindset shifts that need to occur for you to be ready and able to achieve your financial goals, we need to create those goals. I encourage the creation and implementation of S.M.A.R.T. goals which help us see just what it takes to ensure our desires materialize.

S.M.A.R.T. goals are goals that are:
- **S**pecific
- **M**easurable
- **A**ttainable
- **R**ealistic
- **T**ime-bound

For example, "I want to save $50,000" is a desire because it lacks the five attributes of a S.M.A.R.T. goal. However, "I want to save $50,000 within two years, toward my vacation, education and a vehicle purchase, using the money I receive from the settlement and my bi-weekly paycheck," is a S.M.A.R.T. goal.

No doubt you have goals that you want to accomplish. However, are your goals S.M.A.R.T. goals? Use the space below to write your desires, such as, "I want to get out of debt." Then, use the S.M.A.R.T. system to make them into S.M.A.R.T. goals.

Desire:

_____

_____

S.M.A.R.T. goal:

_____

_____

Desire:

_____

_____

S.M.A.R.T. goal:

_____

_____

Desire:

_____

_____

S.M.A.R.T. goal:

_____

_____

Desire:

_____

_____

S.M.A.R.T. goal:

_____

_____

Desire:

_____

S.M.A.R.T. goal:

_____

_____

Review the goals listed above. Are your goals in line with the reasons you purchased this book? If so, you have already taken the first step towards accomplishing your goals. But now, we need to consider what else is necessary to accomplish your goals.

Start by brainstorming. What do you think you need to have, have in place, get rid of, take on, go through, set up, change, learn, unlearn, dismiss, acknowledge, buy, sell, etc., in order for you to accomplish your goals?

For example, you may write: read some personal finance books, save $500 to start, take a class in sewing, photography, or cooking, clean out my garage, have a yard sale to raise some money, get rid of old clothes, set up a reading room or study, make an appointment with a therapist, counselor, or coach, learn more about myself, gain more confidence.

What do you need to further accomplish your goals? Write it in the space below.

_____

_____

_____

_____

_____

_____

_____

Take a look at your list. Circle the ideas that you can begin to implement this week. Of the circled ideas, prioritize the top three. List them below and take action:

1. _____

_____

_____

2. _____

_____

_____

3. _____

_____

_____

Now, you'll simply repeat this process every week. By considering the small steps that are required, you move closer and closer to accomplishing your big goals. The smaller steps also help to reduce any anxiety that may arise and overwhelm. And, you can celebrate the small victories that will lead to your larger success. We all need the small wins to motivate us on our financial journeys.

Money Master Principle #4

Divide savings between regular savings, emergency savings, retirement savings and investment savings (and business savings, if applicable)

Step 7

The 30-Day Look Back

Living paycheck-to-paycheck is a habit developed over time. In order to break that habit and begin to live in abundance, you must acknowledge, assess, and connect your behavior. Then, you must develop a new habit. Your financial choices over the past 30-90 days are the best way to understand why you're having a difficult time making ends meet.

A 30-90 day period is a perfect window of time to assess how you spend your money, and when you spend the most. Just like a probationary period at a new job serves as a time for assessment, so does the 30-day look back. When you better understand your spending behavior, you can do something about it. As I always tell my clients, "The numbers tell a story, and they never lie." So, let's see what story your numbers are telling.

Of course, reviewing your finances in detail requires time, attention, and patience. Try starting with a 30-day look back. (Once you've gained momentum, you may feel inspired to go back further, to 60 or even 90 days.) Starting with 30 days won't overwhelm you, and will provide the information you need to assess your spending behavior. Remember, you're looking for the story being told about your money. Follow these steps to complete your 30-day look back:

STEP 1—Gather information

Collect your bank account and any credit card statements, as well as any receipts for cash you've spent over the past 30 days. If you don't have your statements, you can request copies from your banks and creditors.

STEP 2—Decide how you'll build your tracker

You can create your tracker by hand on graph paper or plain regular paper. You can also create a spreadsheet on your computer or use a notepad or spreadsheet app in your smartphone.

STEP 3—Set up your categories

On paper, or on your computer spreadsheet, create the following categories, in vertical columns:

Food	Transport & Gas	Household Goods	Monthly Bills & Payments	ATM Wthdrwls/ In My Pocket

These are the most common spending categories. As you go through your statements and receipts, if you come across an expense that doesn't fit in any of these categories, simply create a new column for that category. You can also create a miscellaneous column and add the expense there. (This can be especially useful for expenses that don't occur often.)

Step 4—Fill in your tracker

Start with your statements. Enter each transaction amount in your tracker, in its proper category. For example, if you spent $42.05 on gas, you'll enter $42.05 under the transportation category. Do this for each expense, whether paid for with your debit/credit card, cash or by check. Also, don't forget about any transactions you make using PayPal or another processor. Be careful not to duplicate expenses. If you withdraw cash from an ATM, and use that cash to make a purchase, enter only one of those transactions, either the ATM withdrawal or each item purchased with the cash you withdrew, into your tracker. For example, if you withdraw $100 and spend $5.98 on snacks, $35 on household goods, $25.75 at the gas station, have the remaining dollars in your pocket, you could enter this into your tracker one of two ways:

As an ATM withdrawal

Food	Transport & Gas	Household Goods	Monthly Bills & Payments	ATM Wthdrwls/ In My Pocket
				$100

Or as separate transactions with the remaining cash listed in the ATM Withdrawal/In My Pocket column

Master My Money

Food	Transport & Gas	Household Goods	Monthly Bills & Payments	ATM Wthdrwls/ In My Pocket
$5.98	$25.75	$35.00		$33.27

Once you've logged every expense, it's time to add a column for your income. Here, you'll log your paychecks and any other income or deposits you've made over the last 30 days.

Income	Food	Transport & Gas	Household Goods	Monthly Bills & Payments

STEP 5—Add it up

Add the numbers in each category; be sure to use a calculator. Put the total at the bottom of each column.

STEP 6—Take a close look

Let's analyze the numbers. These questions can help you analyze your spending in more detail.

1. In which categories did you spend the most money? (List the top five.)

2. In which categories did you spend the least money? (List the top three.)

3. In which three categories could you most easily reduce your spending?

4. How much more or less did you spend on dining out versus grocery shopping?

5. How much are you spending on average on transportation? How can you reduce that expense?

6. Were most of your bills fixed or variable? Of the variable bills, how many can you reduce?

7. How much income did you have? Expenses?

8. Did you spend more on debts (credit card and store charge cards, student loans, etc.) than you did on other types of bills combined?

9. Are your expenses more than your income?

10. How much did you spend on personal expenses like hair, clothes, shoes, and grooming?

11. Did you put any money into savings or investment accounts? How much?

12. How much did you spend on professional services, like lawyers, accountant, financial coach, photographer, assistant, therapy/counseling, trainer/nutritionist, etc.?

13. How many checks did you write? Is this a normal level of activity?

14. How much have you contributed to charitable organizations?

15. How many ATM withdrawals did you make? Is this a normal level of activity?

STEP 7—Craft your story

Reflect on your answers to these questions, and use them to create a story. Your story should include facts, as revealed by your numbers, but also describe how you feel about your behavior and what you're learning about yourself. It might sound something like this:

"In the past 30 days, I earned $3,800 and spent $3,100. This means I spent less than I made. I spent the most on _____ and the least on _____. I made _____ ATM withdrawals and paid for all my gas using cash (I kept my receipts). I only wrote three checks this month. One bounced because I had to pay a late fee. I receive a paycheck every two weeks and I noticed that I pay more expenses with the second check. I spent $_____ on clothes and shoes. I am disappointed. I can reduce/eliminate expenses altogether in several areas."

Write your story below.

_____

_____

_____

_____

_____

_____

_____

_____
_____
_____
_____
_____
_____
_____
_____
_____
_____
_____
_____
_____
_____
_____
_____
_____

Read your story a few times. How do you feel about what you read? Are you pleased with your spending behavior? Are you surprised by anything you learned?

_____
_____
_____
_____

_____

_____

_____

_____

_____

_____

What is your overall feeling about the exercise you just completed?

_____

_____

_____

_____

_____

Completing your 30-day look back only scratches the surface of your spending behavior. A 60 or 90-day look back better establishes patterns and trends in your spending behavior. Don't be intimidated by the time or patience required to do a 60 or 90-day look back. Once you've gathered the information, it's just a matter of entering it into your tracker.

Challenge Exercise
Conduct a 60 or 90-day look back to learn even more about your spending behavior.

Master My Money

The tracker you've completed and the story you created is a reflection of your past, not a prediction of your future. Don't beat yourself up, and don't be overly proud. While a 60 or 90-day look back will provide more insight, you already have enough information to understand why you're living paycheck-to-paycheck. You've learned where your money is going, and where you need to make improvements to reduce or eliminate expenses. Your financial potential is being suppressed. Your ability to master your money and achieve the financial goals you have set relies on your fortitude and discipline with your everyday financial transactions. You can do this. You can take control of your money. You can utilize the tracking discipline to master your money, and be on your way to wealth building.

Money Master Principle #5

Manage credit and debt responsibly at or below 30% of credit limit

Step 8

Your Current Income and Expenses

While your 30-day look back was based on the past, now we want to look at your expected expenses for the near future. You'll list all of your income and expenses for the upcoming month, and you'll be as exact as possible – no more guesstimates.

In this exploration, you'll account for regular monthly obligations, like your cable bill or rent. If any of your bills are due every other month, use an average of the cost over the last two months. For example, if you pay your electricity bill every other month on the 3rd and the next bill is $150, divide that amount by two, and use the result ($75) for your electricity expense for both months.

If you don't know exactly how much a bill or other expense will be, use the previous month's amount as a base. Once you have listed all of your expenses, you'll shift to your income—be sure to account for all sources of income you receive.

Master My Money
Expenses

Home

Mortgage/Rent	$
Utilities	
Cable	
Internet	
Cell phone	
Homeowner/Renter's Insurance	
Other	
Other	
Total Home Expenses	$

Daily Living

Groceries	$
Dining out	
Fast food	
Beverages	
Alcohol	
Laundry/Dry cleaning	
Gas/Fuel	
Other	
Total Daily Living Expenses	$

Transportation

Car payment	$
Car insurance	
Shared Car/Rental	
Cab/Taxi	
Public Transportation	
Parking	
Airplane	
Train	
Other	
Other	
Total Transportation Expenses	$

Entertainment

Party	$
DVD/Video	
Movies/Plays	
Concerts	
Festivals	
Other	
Other	
Total Entertainment Expenses	$

Health

Health club/Gym	$
Health insurance	
Prescriptions	
Over-the-counter drugs	
Co-pays	
Life Insurance	
Pet care	
Other	
Other	
Total Health Expenses	$

Business/Vacation

Lodging	$
Airplane/Train	
Rental car	
Food	
Email/Website	
Marketing	
Rent	
Business phone	

Other	
Total Business/Vacation Expenses	$

Dues/Subscriptions

Magazines/Books	$
Newspaper	
Memberships	
Associations	
Tithes	
Charity	
Other	
Other	
Total Dues/Subscriptions Expenses	$

Personal

Clothes	$
Shoes	
Accessories	
Salon/Barber	
Grooming	
Pampering	
Other	
Total Personal Expenses	$

Financial

Loans	$
Credit card payments	
Bank fees	
Income taxes	
Medical debt	
Checks	
ATM Withdrawals	
Other	
Other	
Total Financial Expenses	$

Children/Elder Care

Daycare	$
Overnight care	
Babysitter	
Activities	
Supplies/Materials	
Clothing and shoes	
Health	
Toys/Gifts	
Other	

Other	
Total Children/Elder Care Expenses	$

Total Expenses

Total Home Expenses	$
Total Daily Living Expenses	
Total Transportation Expenses	
Total Entertainment Expenses	
Total Health Expenses	
Total Business/Vacation Expenses	
Total Dues/Subscription Expenses	
Total Personal Expenses	
Total Financial Expenses	
Total Children/Elder Care Expenses	
Grand Total Expenses	$

Income

Salary/Wages	$
Bonus	
Part-time job	
Pension	
Interest/Dividends	
Deposits	
Child support	
Alimony	
SSI	
Disability	
Business income	
Other	
Other	
Total Income	$

In this exercise, you created a detailed view of your financial life. It shows exactly where you spend your money every month. Many people who have financial frustrations complain that they simply don't know where their money goes each month. They just know they paid bills and bought groceries, and the rest seemed to disappear. But now, you're armed with specific, accurate information. You've detailed your income and expenses, and you know exactly where your money is going so you can answer this central question:

Are you living within or outside of your means?

Challenge Exercise

Calculate your net income.

To determine your net income, subtract your total expenses from your total income. If your net income is a positive number, you're living within your means. If your net income is a negative number, you're living outside your means.

Net Income

Total Income	$
Less: Total Expenses	
Net Income	$

I am living _____ of my means.

How do you feel about this statement? Write your thoughts below.

_____

_____

_____

_____

_____

Even if you're living within your means, it's always a good idea to reduce or eliminate expenses where you can. Put a check next to the expenses you want to reduce or eliminate. We'll come back to those later.

When it comes to changing your financial life, it begins and ends with your income and expenses. In most cases, you can either increase your income or decrease your expenses—doing both is difficult. Doing one of these (or a combination of both, if you can) will allow you to adjust your spending behavior.

Feel like you're always paying bills? That's probably because you have too many. Reduce and eliminate as much as you can. Start with reductions, and then move to eliminations. If you can eliminate any expenses altogether, you should. Remember you're on your way to unlocking your financial potential. The key to doing that is understanding the realities of your income and expenses, and taking action.

Of course, it's certainly possible to increase your income, but that usually takes more time. Reducing your expenses is something you can start immediately – today. Nevertheless, when it comes to increasing your income, you can consider the following possibilities:

- Secure a second job or per diem work

- Start a business based on a hobby or talent that you can profit from

- Buy or buy into an established business with proven profitability

- Setup an online business for an in-demand product

- Outsource your skills on sites like Fiverr.com

- Sell items on EBay or Amazon

- Become a consultant or speaker in your area of expertise

- Do odd jobs for people in your network

- Explore mystery shopping and paid surveys

- Invest in stocks that pay dividends and bonds that pay interest

- Explore investing in real estate, specifically in rental income properties

- Host classes or educational development courses in your area of expertise

Your wealth foundation depends on both your income and expenses. It is important that you are aware of your total expenses and income so that you are able to increase or decrease in the areas that need the most attention. Dealing with your expenses first will help improve your awareness, and also instill discipline into your financial life. When you can mediate your spending, you will know how to manage the money you receive or earn from any additional income streams.

Money Master Principle #6

Review credit report at least twice a year and know credit score from at least one bureau at any given moment

Step 9

Track Your Spending

You've already reviewed your past spending behavior in the 30-day look back. And, you've examined your present income and expenses. Now, we want to look at your day-to-day spending habits. You'll do this by tracking your spending.

Tracking is a great way to gain control of your spending and learn more about your financial behavior. It provides insight into your spending triggers and daily financial habits. Tracking can also reveal things you didn't know about yourself, and that can be life-changing.

I've had clients who hated the idea of tracking at first. The thought of carrying a notepad and jotting down everything they bought every day seemed like too much work. However, once they accepted the challenge and began tracking, they realized its true power. Some things you'll notice about tracking are:

- It only takes a couple of days to get into the habit of logging your expenses.

- It can easily become a habit that you maintain beyond two weeks.
- You'll think about your purchases more carefully before making them.
- You may find you even forego some purchases because you don't want to write them down.

So how do you track your expenses? It's simple. Gather a pen/pencil and a small pocket notepad. Every time you spend money (whether by credit card, debit card, cash or check) write it in the notepad. Record the name and price of the item. For example, "coffee - $1.75" or "electric bill - $76.32" or "lunch - $9.89."

At the end of each day, add all your purchases and write the total at the bottom of that day's page. Track each day's expenses until you've tracked for a full week.

At the end of the week, review all the expenses from each day, and create categories. For example, "lunch" and "coffee" expenses will go under "food and beverages," and "electric bill" will go in the "bills" category. Create your categories based on the types of expenses you incur. List the amount of each expense under each category. Add them up to create a total.

Challenge Exercise
Track your spending for the next seven days.

It's okay if you forget and fall off the wagon. Just remember to get back on track.

Now assess your spending for the week. In which category did you spend the most? The least? Do you have any expenses that occur daily? What are they? Were you pleased with your spending over the weekend?

_____

_____

_____

_____

What else have you learned after tracking for one week?

_____

_____

_____

_____

It's a good idea to track your spending for two full weeks. You'll learn more about your spending behavior, get a clear view of your spending during the week versus on the weekend, see how you spend outside of work hours, and understand what you spend the most and least on during the week.

By now, you should be much more aware of your day-to-day spending habits. When you're aware, you can see the areas where you need to improve and then take action.

Master My Money

Money Master Principle #7

Establish proper protection documents and coverage to protect the foundation being built

Step 10

Your Savings Rate

A savings rate is simply the percentage you set aside out of every dollar you earn. While it's not the only method, setting a target savings rate is an effective way to save.

Ideally, you want to start saving at least 10% of your income. However, if you've never saved before or have difficulty saving your money, creating the habit of saving consistently— regardless of the amount—is more important than saving a specific percentage.

If you're already saving, we can calculate your savings rate. But first, an example: Let's say you make $1,000 and save $75 every month. Divide $75 by $1,000, to get .075. This means you save $0.075 cents for every $1 you earn. Multiply by 100% and you get a savings rate of 7.5%. This means you're saving 7.5% of your after-tax income.

Your monthly savings	
÷ Your monthly income (after taxes)	
= Your savings rate (decimal)	
* 100	
= Your savings rate (percent)	

If you aren't saving, now is the time to start. Here's how:

1. Calculate your net income: Your total income less your total expenses equals your net income. If your net income is negative, it's time to review your expenses to determine what you can reduce or eliminate to get a positive net income. (See Chapter 8 for more information.)

2. Once you have a positive net income, you can decide how much of it you want to save. For example, if your total monthly income after taxes is $2,500 and your net income is $288, and you choose to save $150, you'll use $150 to determine your saving rate.

3. Divide the amount of savings by the total income. Going back to our example, $150/$2,500 = 0.06. For every $1 of income earned you are saving $0.06.

Remember, you're saving this amount after all of your expenses are paid. Ideally, you want to think of your savings as a regular expense, just like any other monthly bill. To do that, go back to the page where the expenses are and add savings to the financial obligation section. You've now added a savings strategy to your budget and are practicing the golden rule of budgeting. After you've started saving, work to increase the amount in small increments. A good goal to work toward is 10% of your total income.

It's important to begin to put yourself first, financially. And that means saving. All it takes is a review of your expenses to see how you can spend less, and save more.

"Don't be afraid to invest in yourself. Looking at the master budget can be challenging at first, but Dominiqué was there to empower me every step of the way. Soon I realized one small step led to another and before long I wiped out debt that had been keeping me stressed for years!"

—Sandra (New York)

Money Master Sandra

Sandra was the client you wanted to see succeed. She was a hard-working woman, mother and wife. She always put others before herself. She would give her last to help her family without a doubt. However, it was this mindset that kept Sandra far from accomplishing her financial goals. Her lack of financial discipline contributed to the outcomes she was experiencing: little to no savings to cover life's emergencies, mounting debt, paycheck to paycheck living, stress from worrying about her money situation and an overall deep-seated anxiety about her financial future. First thing first, we worked on Sandra's mindset, where I coached her about the golden rule in budgeting, paying yourself first! She deserved it. She worked hard for her money and it was time that it showed. Next we shifted to balancing her budget and getting a good understanding on where she stood with respect to her creditors, including the family members she borrowed from. I constructed an aggressive debt reduction strategy in conjunction with an intense savings strategy. Sandra saw results quickly! She got so motivated because her system of saving and debt reduction was working. For once, she saw her hard-earned money adding up. She was gaining the control she needed, to run her financial life instead of it running her. Sandra's plight went from despair to dynamic in weeks, with a sure-fire strategy to save her thousands, while paying off thousands; a true win-win situation.

Step 11

Your Debt Review

Living paycheck-to-paycheck and feeling financially challenged is often the result of too much debt. Debt has a way of hanging over our heads, so much so that we'll spend our last penny to make a payment. And then, we eagerly await our next check to pay off more debt. Of course, no one wants to owe money to anyone. But when we do, the safest and most effective way to deal with it is to create a payment strategy that we can afford, stick to, and feel good about. When we can't stick to our debt repayment terms, we stress and lose credibility with our creditors.

What if you loaned money to someone, they paid back half the loan, and you never heard from them again? Would you loan them money a second time? Creditors view you in the same way. So it's important to create a payment plan you can stick to. When you feel comfortable with a debt repayment strategy, you're less likely to feel stressed, or complain about making payments. You borrowed the money; you have to pay it back. And by doing it right, you're demonstrating you're a responsible borrower and consumer.

109

Now, it's time to look at all of your debt, and how much it's costing you in both interest and time.

STEP 1
Gather all your debt statements.

STEP 2
Use the statements to complete the following chart:

Name of Creditor	Due Date	Interest Rate	Balance Owed	Monthly Payment Amount

Several schools of thoughts exist about how to reduce debt. These are the three I feel are most effective:

1. **Pay whatever feels comfortable to you**. No matter how you approach your debt reduction plan, if it doesn't feel good to you, you're less likely to stick to it.

2. **Pay the debt with the highest interest rate first**. When appropriate, paying down or paying off the debt with the highest interest rate is the best choice if your budget is sensitive to the cost of interest. Higher interest rate debt costs more over time. The interest charged against the amount you've borrowed can accumulate quickly from month to month.

3. **Pay the lowest balance first**. This can be the best strategy if it's important for you to see progress on paying down debt as soon as possible. Some of us need small successes right away to provide encouragement and motivation to stay focused. If you

can manage the higher interest rates of other debts in exchange for paying off a lower balance sooner, it can be worthwhile.

Which method feels the best for you and fits your current personal financial situation the best? If you choose to pay debt with the lowest balance or highest interest rate, follow these steps:

1. Rank your debts from the highest interest rate to lowest interest rate, or the lowest balance to highest balance.

2. Review the minimum amount due each month for the top three. Are you making at least the minimum payments?

3. If you are, make a commitment to pay more than the monthly minimum. Increase the payment $5-$100.

4. If you're not making the minimum payment amount, bump up your payments to the minimum. But review your expenses first. Revisit the last chapter and see which expenses you identified with a check mark that could be reduced or eliminated. You can then shift funds from these expenses to the debt payment.

NOTE: If you have medical debt that isn't accumulating interest, always make just the minimum payments. Because you aren't being charged interest there's no benefit to paying it off before other debts. Make a payment arrangement that's affordable based on your income and expenses, and pay that debt until you increase income or decrease expenses enough to increase those payments, or pay off the debt entirely.

If, after adding up your debts, you find that the total monthly debt payment is more than 50% of your income, you'll want to consider making new payment arrangements. You can do this by calling your creditor and negotiating for a reduced payment or lower interest rate.

Unless you're comfortable with this debt-to-income ratio, you will want to make new payment arrangements. While lowering payments may increase the time it takes to pay off the debt, it may also provide short-term relief and lessen the burden on your budget. As long as you fully understand the consequences of your actions, you will be making an informed decision that you can feel confident about.

When increasing a monthly payment amount, you'll want to boost it by at least the amount of your interest charge. Then, when you make a payment or minimum payment, the interest for that month is deducted from the payment and the balance is applied to your principal. Since payments are applied this way, your payments don't necessarily reduce the actual amount you owe. For example, if your interest is $25 and you make a $75 payment on a $1,000 balance, only $50 is being applied to the balance, making it $950. However, if you increase your payment by $25 to $100, $25 goes to interest and $75 is applied to the balance, making it $925 after your payment.

When you've reduced a balance to at least 30% of your credit limit, you should consider modifying the payment based on your budget. If you can afford to make the increased payments, do so. If you can increase the payments by more, you should. However, if you reduce the payment, feel good about it. Because you've already saved on interest due to the increased payments you already made. And, you've reduced the debt repayment period, or length of time that you would have to make payments before the debt is paid off. When you pay off a debt, shift the payment amount you were making to the next debt in your list, based on the highest rate or the lowest balance.

Money Master Principle #8

Organize financial documents regularly and keep tidy records.

Master My Money

Step 12

Your Credit Review

Your credit profile is important and for several reasons. Today, you need credit just to get a job or find a place to live, rent a car, get a cell phone or get your gas turned on. When you have less than excellent credit, you pay for it in the form of higher interest rates and/or required deposits.

As we mentioned earlier, there are three major credit bureaus: Experian, Equifax and TransUnion. When they develop a score for your profile and behavior, it is based on the following factors:

Factor	% of Score
Payment History Do you pay on time?	35%
Utilization of Credit How much you owe	30%
Length of Payment History How long you've been building credit	15%
New Credit Do you apply for credit frequently?	10%
Mix of Credit Do you have a variety of credit?	10%

I suggest that you pull your credit reports from AnnualCreditReport.com. You can do this via phone, mail or online.

To get your report, follow these steps:

1. Visit AnnualCreditReport.com.

2. Choose your state.

3. Click "Request your free credit reports."

4. Click "Request your credit report."

5. Follow the on-screen instructions.

To request your credit report by phone:
Call 1.877.322.8228
Follow the verification process as specified. Your reports will be mailed to you within fifteen days. Allow two to three weeks for delivery.

To request your credit report by mail:
Download the request form at
AnnualCreditReport.com/ManualRequestForm.action
Print and complete the form.
Mail the completed form to
     Annual Credit Report Request Service
     P.O. Box 105281
     Atlanta, GA 30348-5281
Your reports will be mailed to you within fifteen days. Allow two to three weeks for delivery.

If you have trouble or are unable to access your free reports from annualcreditreport.com, you can still access reports, scores, and other information for free by visiting the websites below. You will not need a credit card in order to access your reports and/or scores:

1. CreditKarma.com provides a free credit report from TransUnion.

2. Quizzle.com provides a free Equifax report and Vantage Score 3.0. (Vantage Scores range from 300-850.)

3. Credit.com provides an Experian National Equivalency Score (360-840) and Vantage Score 3.0. While you won't get a full credit report, you can get a credit report card, which gives you a grade (A-F) on each area of your credit that determines your score.

4. CreditSesame.com provides your Experian National Equivalency Score.

Once you receive your reports, review them meticulously for accuracy. The Federal Trade Commission published a study in late December 2012 which stated that one out of every five consumers has an error on the credit report. That could be you! We want to give this exercise ample attention because any errors that you report or dispute could positively affect your credit score.

Here are some strategies for reviewing your credit reports:

- Set aside at least an hour to review each report.
- Read every page of the report.
- Make note of your name, report number and the date of the report which are necessary for any disputes.

Start your review by checking the accuracy of the following:

- Confirm that the following personal information is correct:
  - ☐ Names and spellings
  - ☐ Addresses
  - ☐ Year of birth
  - ☐ Phone numbers
  - ☐ Former and current employers
- Notices
- Familiar names of creditor
- Accurate account numbers
- Dates opened
- Monthly payments (if reported)
- Credit limits
- Status of the account
- Creditor's comments/notes/statements
- Payment history
- Consider hard and soft inquiries to see with whom your credit history has been shared

If you find ANY inaccuracies, make a detailed note so that you can prepare a dispute. If you have any questions about a specific account listed on any of your reports, write your question next to the account.

Once you've reviewed each report, call the respective bureau and speak to a representative about any questions you have. If necessary, ask the representative for specific instruction for filing a dispute.

You can reach the credit bureaus at:

Experian
Consumer Assistance
P.O. Box 2002
Allen, TX 75013

Equifax
P.O. Box 740241
Atlanta, GA 30374

TransUnion
P.O. Box 2000
Chester, PA 19022

You can also use this sample letter when disputing items your credit report:

Master My Money

Date:

John Doe (First, middle, last, Jr./Sr.)
12345 Your Street
City, State, Zip
Social Security#:

Credit Bureau Name
Address
City, State, Zip

Re: Notice of dispute pursuant to Section 611 of the Federal Fair Credit Reporting Act

To Whom It May Concern:

I recently obtained a copy of my consumer's credit report from your bureau and hereby dispute the completeness and accuracy of the following information. This information is injurious to my consumer report and I request that you correct this information immediately. The information I am disputing is as follows:
Please remove this inaccurate information from my credit report and update my records.

I have never lived at this address: _____.

This account does not belong to me. Please remove it from my files and your records and/or show me proof of such account belonging to me: _____

Account name and number

Master My Money

Please remove this account from my records as it contains inaccurate/outdated information: _____

Account name and number

My consumer report is extremely valuable to me. Please be advised that willful non-compliance is a violation of the Federal Fair Credit Reporting Act. I assume thirty (30) days is a reasonable amount of time for your investigation unless I am notified otherwise. Upon resolution of this dispute, please provide me with an updated credit report.

Respectfully,
[Your Signature]

Money Master Principle #9

Read money and wealth-related materials at least once a week

Step 13

Your Protection Review

When it comes to your money, protection is defined as insurance, estate planning, health proxies and advance directives.

Let's start with insurance. Your answers to the questions in the *Your Current Financial Situation Chapter* indicate the actions you need to take for specific types of protection.

Life Insurance

Many people have life insurance through their employer, but don't know the details of their coverage. If this is you, then you have some homework to do:

- Research your employee benefit policy for life insurance

- What kinds of coverage do you have? What is the benefit amount?

- If something were to happen to you, how does your family file a claim or take action on the policy?

- Print the pages that describe the coverage, and make sure you have current contact information.

If you do not have life insurance, are under covered or need to adjust your coverage, then you should seek a professional insurance agent. While it can be quite easy to find an agent, you may want to ask a family member or friend for a referral. Remember, this is a financial relationship. So you want to ensure you have the right fit.

Lastly, be sure that you don't have too much coverage. Websites like <u>DinkyTown.com</u> offer life insurance calculators that help assess your insurance needs. Once you calculate your needs, you can circle back with your insurance agent to move forward. Together, you should be able to further evaluate your need, compare it to existing coverage, and make any modifications, if necessary. Be sure you are comfortable with any proposed changes, and that you can afford them, according to your budget. Don't be pressured into anything that doesn't feel right. If you do feel pressure, simply take a day or more to sleep on the details, seek a second opinion, or do your own research. Then resume discussions about moving forward. Your agent should not have any objections to this approach. If he or she does, consider finding another agent.

Car Insurance

The car insurance landscape is highly competitive, so you have opportunities to secure affordable coverage. Be sure to comparison shop. If, after considering your expenses, car insurance is one that you can reduce, do some research and shop for a new quote. But be sure not to jeopardize your coverage.

Renter's Insurance

Renter's insurance is a must for anyone who doesn't own his or her home. Minimal coverage is quite inexpensive: about $10-$20 a month. As inexpensive as it can be, renter's insurance is very important. If you were robbed today, would you be able to replace all your belongings tomorrow, using the money you have in your checking or savings account? If the answer is no, then you should consider renter's insurance, with no hesitation. If the answer is yes, then you should still consider it to minimize your out-of-pocket expenses. Be sure that your policy includes theft coverage, and inquire about flood, fire, earthquake, and other types of protection.

Business Insurance

If you are an entrepreneur or business owner, you'd want to have some form of business or liability insurance. You can consult your life insurance agent about the types of business insurance available. When you own your own business, you can never be too safe. Protecting yourself and your business is important to your sustainability and livelihood. In the event that you are sued, or have to pay for damages of some sort, you'll have insurance to access. Be sure you understand what your unique business needs are, choose coverage that meets those needs.

Living Will

Your living will is a document used to direct your medical/health care wishes, in the event that you cannot speak for yourself. You can learn more about creating these documents at Nolo.com. While creating these documents can be inexpensive, it can be very important to your financial and physical wellbeing.

Will, Living Trust & Durable Financial Power of Attorney

Your will is a document that outlines your final wishes. It is simple to create on your own, but also can be drafted by an attorney. Your living trust is an arrangement for managing your property and assets. Because this type of trust is set up while you are still alive, you'll maintain control of your assets and properties within the trust until your death. At that time, your named trustee will take over management of the trust. Lastly, your durable financial power of attorney is an individual who you name to manage your financial affairs in the event you become incapacitated. Because, this type of arrangement is "durable," you'll state if you want it to take effect now, or only in the event you become incapacitated.

Having these documents in place now can save your family headaches and arguments in the future. You will have specified how you want your affairs, property, and assets managed, and you can feel confident your wishes will be carried out according to your instructions. You can learn more about each type of protection and how to employ them at <u>Nolo.com</u>.

Part of having your financial house in order is protecting it. You don't want to build it and then lose it all. So, take action now by seeking the appropriate professionals, conducting interviews, learning about their offerings, understanding your needs, and securing the appropriate protections.

Master My Money

Step 14

Weekly Budgeting

You've probably noticed that we haven't discussed budgeting yet. And you might be okay with that. Budgeting tends to be a less-popular pastime for most. It's often associated with lots of detail, complicated spreadsheets, and unpleasant limits on spending. While some of that is true, budgeting is about much more.

As we approach the subject, it's important to remember you're after something greater; your "Why Now." Your mission is to find the holes and stop the leaks in your personal financial situation; to build a solid wealth foundation that you can be confident will support your financial future; and to stop living paycheck-to-paycheck. You've been managing your money the same way for quite some time. So, adopting new methods and building new habits may not come easily, and may require some sacrifice.

Your budget can be your ally. It gives insight into your money story. It can tell you exactly what you can afford to do and what you can't. That awareness leads to more confident decisions about money. And that's a valuable form of financial freedom.

You can create your budget on a computer spreadsheet, using special budgeting software, or with simple pen and paper. Choose the method that's most comfortable for you.

Since no longer living in financial bondage is your goal, it's a good idea to begin with a weekly budget. Once you've gained insight and built discipline, you can shift to a bi-weekly or monthly budget. You'll learn a lot about your financial behavior and money story by budgeting on a weekly basis. Here's how to get started:

Make a list of all of your regular expenses, with their amounts and due dates. You can reference your expense list from the earlier chapter if that is helpful. But be sure to make a separate list.

Rewrite those expenses by due date, with the earliest first. Next to the expense, write the day of the month the expense is due.

Think about your next two paychecks (if you are paid bi-weekly or every other week) or next month's check (if you are paid monthly). Given the dates you will get paid, which check (the first or the second) will cover each expense? You should be able to review the expenses by date (remember, if they aren't listed by due date, rewrite them according to due date, in chronological order). Draw a line under the last expense that can be paid with your first check. All expenses above the line should be paid with that check. All expenses below that line will be paid with the second check.

Add up all the expenses for the first paycheck and then for the second. Do your expenses exceed your income for each period? If so, it's time to consider a few things:

1. Can you reduce any payments?

2. Can you change the due date for any expenses?

3. Because it's unlikely your income will increase soon enough to cover these expenses, you should explore these options to make the budget work for you.

4. If you're tracking your daily spending, you have additional insight into your true expenses. You have both expected expenses, with due dates, in addition to day-to-day expenses. At the end of each "tracking week," analyze what you've spent. Are you on track to spend less than your budget for this pay period? Or will you have spent nearly everything by the time the next paycheck arrives? Have you set aside any savings yet?

5. If you're tracking on a daily basis, then you'll need to analyze your bank account activity at the end of the week, create categories, total the expenses in each category, and include those categories on your budget sheet. You'll simply add the next week's total expenses to each category.

By simultaneously tracking your spending and analyzing your monthly expenses, you'll learn:

- When your bills are due

- Which paycheck will cover which expenses

- Whether you can afford your expenses

- How much you spend on expected expenses compared to day-to-day expenses

- Which categories of day-to-day expenses can be reduced

- How your savings plan is being affected by your spending

- Whether you can spend money on a latte, new outfit, new shoes, dinner out, a weekend getaway, a loan to a friend or anything else

What you learn from creating and following a budget will definitely affect your money mindset, your behavior and your outcomes. You'll gain discipline. You'll see opportunities to modify your finances, so they work for you and your family. You'll increase your focus and gain momentum toward your goals.

"My intentional focus is to continue to make my money work for me and continue to educate myself in financial literacy."

—Kevin (California)

Money Master Kevin

Kevin was young and not very interested in budgeting at all. He made good money as an engineer for the city of Long Beach, but wanted to learn more about money and investing. Kevin became a client and hated it! He hated tracking; he hated budgeting and simply didn't like the manual labor of managing his money. However, he LOVED my Excel budget! See, Kevin was familiar with spreadsheets and he became very familiar with the custom one I built for him. Before I knew it, Kevin was reporting good progress on his debt and savings. He allowed the budget to work for him, to tell him what he could afford to do; to show him the opportunities to take advantage of. About one year later, using the budget I had built for him, Kevin had substantially reduced debt, significantly increased savings and was ready to purchase a home. He saved thousands of dollars for a down payment, purchased his first home before the age of twenty-five and less than two years later sold it for a profit of $60,000! It all began with constant coaching from me, encouraging Kevin to update his budget, a custom budget and Kevin's desire to succeed. That's it.

Master My Money

Step 15

Set Up Online Banking and Auto Debit

Now that you've written out all of your expenses, you can boost your financial efficiency by setting up automatic payments. Typically, you can do this either through your bank's online bill pay service, or through each payee's website.

I recommend using your bank's online bill pay service whenever possible. This enables you to manage more expenses from one place, giving you greater control over your total financial picture.

Contact your bank to learn more about online bill pay. Be sure to ask when the money is drafted, and if payments are made electronically, or if they will send actual checks to your payees. If they do send checks, find out when the funds will be withdrawn from your checking account, and when the payee will receive the check.

Automating your expenses is a great way to ensure your bills are always paid on time, without too much work, and without stamps. Essentially, this is your system, put in place to do the work for you. You only need to check in on the system regularly to be sure it's running properly.

You may be hesitant to set up your system because of fears about overdrawing your account or not having money in the account. However, those are the worries we have left behind. With your new mindset, your new approach, and your new understanding about your money, you can be confident that you will have enough to cover your obligations. Now, you will be able to rest knowing you're not overdrawing your account.

In the case you do come up short, you can simply transfer money from your savings to your checking. That is why we started saving, even while paying down debts and regular bills. To fully take control of your financial life, you must have that cushion.

Money Master Principle #10

Educate and share with others what you know about money and building wealth

Master My Money

Step 16

Work with a Professional

The right professional can help you explore your money mindsets and basic financial challenges even more effectively. While there are many types of financial professionals, I've found that it's important to find the right fit for your needs. Just because a Financial Advisor or Financial Planner says they can help, doesn't mean they're the best choice.

No doubt you've heard of Financial Advisors. But what are they, exactly? In general, Financial Advisors are licensed and regulated practitioners who work with clients who already have an established wealth foundation of some kind. While this means the client usually has some level of debt they may want to manage, they typically also have a significant level of savings, some assets, such as a home, an investment account, retirement savings, and possibly more. The goal is usually to grow what they already have.

Financial Advisors typically don't work with clients on more basic tasks like creating a budget, reducing debt, and saving for an emergency fund. In my past experience as an Advisor, I tended to focus on investment management, retirement planning and college planning with my clients. My clients generally had six-figure salaries and a substantial amount of investable assets.

Lastly, Financial Advisors are paid a percentage of the assets they manage for you. So, if you're not at a point where you have assets to be managed, a different type of financial professional is likely a better fit for your needs.

A Financial Planner can help with more of the basic elements of your financial life. Planners may or may not be Certified Financial Planners. Just because a professional has a CFP designation, doesn't mean they are the right fit for your needs. You should still conduct an interview and other due diligence to determine if they are the right choice.

A Financial Planner might charge a flat fee for a specific service, or bill an hourly rate. However, you still may not get exactly what you're looking for. Financial Planners use a "holistic" approach to money management. That approach typically includes retirement, college savings, investments, estate planning, tax planning, and insurance planning. While this is very similar to the work a Financial Advisor does, a Financial Planner's clients are generally more "middle class." This can mean they have an annual income of up to $150,000, a five- to six-figure debt load, a low to moderate amount of savings, "decent" credit, and some insurance need(s).

So, who can you turn to if your needs are more basic? That's where professionals like me come into play. We're known as Financial Coaches, or Professional Daily Money Managers, and our numbers are increasing. I consider myself to be a Personal Financial Coach and Strategist, and I work with both individuals and companies.

Financial Coaches and Daily Money Managers help clients with basic financial needs, such as budgeting, debt reduction, savings and spending plans, living within their means, paying bills efficiently, reconciling accounts, restoring and improving credit, and financial education.

While Financial Coaches and Daily Money Managers don't typically focus on investing, we may be able to address some investment, retirement and college saving, and insurance needs. While this can depend on whether we hold certain licenses or not, many of us simply choose not to offer these services. (We're always happy to refer clients to other professionals within our networks who do offer them.)

Financial Coaches and Daily Money Managers typically have more flexible and affordable fees than Financial Advisors and Financial Planners. We may charge an hourly rate, ranging from $35-$250 per hour, depending on the individual situation and the services needed. We also may offer packages or programs at flat rates, with flexible payment plans, as I do. This can be a good option for clients with basic financial needs that span several areas, such as debt, savings, credit, and budgeting. In these cases, a client can have all areas addressed over a specific period of time, for a flat fee. These situations offer complete transparency, with no surprises.

Before you commit to working with a financial professional there are a few questions you should ask, in order to get to know them better, understand how they work with their clients, and determine if they meet your financial needs. The answers to these questions will ultimately, help you determine if there is a "good fit."

Remember, this interview is valuable because it could be the beginning of a relationship with someone you will need to trust with your financial future. If you feel comfortable with the answers you receive, consider working with this professional. However, be sure to interview at least two other professionals in the same field, so that you're able to compare their responses.

1. How long have you been practicing in this profession?

2. What are your specialties or areas of expertise?

3. Are you licensed? By whom? Do you hold any designations? If so, which ones?

4. How do you work with your clients? How often would we be in touch?

5. Given my needs, what type of strategy or plan of action would you suggest?

6. What is your availability? Who would I contact in your absence?

7. Are there any minimum fees to work with you? What about any other requirements?

8. What do your clients like most about working with you?

9. What happens if I am not satisfied with the service you provide?

10. How are you paid? How often are you paid?

Master My Money

Conclusion

What a journey, right?

First, let me congratulate you on completing this process. Putting your financial house in order can be quite overwhelming, but you did it. You completed the steps, read the book and made progress toward money mastery. I welcome you into our community of wealth builders and money masters. You covered the six core areas of your financial life, and took a deep dive into each, so that you could strengthen that area and create a solid foundation for wealth.

Remember, the goal of this process is to move forward in your financial life with confidence. Confidence knowing your obligations are taken care of, and you don't have to sweat the small stuff. Now, you can simply make informed financial decisions without insecurity. You are also now prepared for emergencies and can be proud that you are now saving. You have a debt strategy in place, you've taken a closer look at your credit profile, and you've assessed your insurance position. You did this!

As you can see, you have devoted a great deal of time and energy to making all of this happen. Your effort is duly noted, and will continue to pay off. I want to remind you however, that there will be times when you "fall off." You might pause your tracking, lose your grip on your expenses and bills, and start to overspend again. But the difference now is, you know how to stop the bleeding. You have the strategies and the discipline. In this case, you'll simply start tracking again, until you are back in control.

You are in charge of your money. Not the other way around. You must always remember that. You are a master of your money, not a slave to your money.

You are equipped with the right tools to have built a secure foundation. What does that mean to you now? To me, it has always meant that, if an emergency occurs or I have a financial unexpectancy, I don't have to worry. I can cover it. My foundation is protected, and I don't have to worry that I will need to rob Peter to pay Paul, to satisfy that unexpectancy. I don't have to live paycheck to paycheck to meet that need. Instead, I can tap my emergency savings, or use that credit card that is "only for emergencies."

It's time to worry less, live more, and be confident about your financial house. Because now, that house sits on a foundation you can always strengthen with the specialized tools and skills you've successfully mastered.

Congratulations!

About the Author

Dr. Dominiqué Reese, owner of Reese Financial Services and creator of Master My Money™, has more than ten years of experience in the financial services industry. She worked on Wall Street as a financial advisor for Merrill Lynch. She managed millions of dollars as the junior partner and financial planning specialist.

Known as The Money Master, her expertise as a personal finance coach and strategist has taken her across the nation. Dr. Reese develops women leaders, executives and business owners into money masters who not only strengthen their financial foundation, but improve their relationship with money to advance their financial literacy.

Dr. Reese has a degree in economics from Princeton University and an honorary doctorate of philosophy from Global Oved Dei Seminary & University.

ReeseFinancialServices.com

Twitter: @Reesefinancial

Facebook: Reese Financial Services

LinkedIn: Dr. Dominique Reese

Master My Money Services

Master My Money™ Monthly Mastermind Club
The ideal way to invest in your financial future and gain discipline, education, moneymaking ideas, motivation and a community of wealth builders and other money masters to promote your money mastery.

Master My Money™ Makeover
A private 6-hour strategy and solution intensive with Dr. Dominique' to drive awareness, action and results in your financial life. This financial makeover will solve your most worrisome money problems and put you on track to reach your full financial potential. 90 days of accountability follow after the makeover.

Master My Money™ 20-Day Financial Reset Challenge
This 20-day challenge is designed to get your mind right, so you can get your money right. In this challenge you will set and reset your thoughts, words and actions about money to create stability and success in your financial life.

Master My Money™ Girlfriend's Makeover
This Makeover is for a group of women (3-10) who want to get their financial house in order TOGETHER! Women spend together, so this makeover allows women to save together. Conducted in the privacy of a comfortable, intimate setting, each woman will have her financial life transformed during the session and receive 1-on-1 coaching with Dr. Dominique'. 30 days of accountability follow after the makeover.

To book Dr. Dominique' or to order additional copies of Master My Money

Master My Money™

1127 W. 45th Street

Los Angeles, CA 90037

213.787.4399

ReeseFinancialServices.com

* *

Please mail _____ copies of

Master My Money™

Name
_____

Address
_____

City / State / Zip

(_____)_____

Phone
_____

Email

Quantity	Price Per Book	Total
	$17.95	
Sales Tax (CA residents add $1.62 or 9% per book)		
Shipping ($3.49 first book, $0.99 each additional)		
Grand Total* (Payable to: Reese Financial)		

* Certified check and money orders only

Also Available on   Amazon.com

153

Master My Money

Master My Money

Made in the USA
Middletown, DE
15 April 2023

28883491R00088